This journal belongs to

_____

TPD PUBLISHING

NIGHTLIGHT. Copyright © 2020 by Kristin Santizo. All rights reserved. No part of this book may be used or reproduced in any manner whatsoever without written permission except in the case of brief quotations in the context of critical articles or reviews.

ISBN: 978-1-7352907-0-6

Unless otherwise indicated, all Scripture quotations are taken from The Holy Bible, the
KING JAMES VERSION (KJV): KING JAMES VERSION, public domain.
Scripture quotations marked (ASV) are taken from THE AMERCIAN STANDARD VERSION BIBLE: AMERICAN STANDARD VERSION, public domain.

Cover and interior design by Oscar Martinez

Dear Child of God,

This book started from the sense that God was asking me to write a journal of His promises for those who are grieving. I am a nurse who worked the ER and High-risk Labor & Delivery. Growing up, our family business was funeral directing. I remember my parents telling me from as early as I can remember that death is a natural part of life, and, if done well, it can be a very beautiful and honorable experience. Always knowing and resting in the knowledge that we will see our loved ones again, and this is just a temporary goodbye.

God loves us and gives us promise after promise of His love towards us. My prayer is that this journal is a continuation of His promises to you. I pray this journal shines like a nightlight to you in a very dark place of grief and loss. I pray that God's promises shine and radiate light in the dark and fill your heart with His everlasting love!

With blessings and love,
- Kristin

NIGHT LIGHT

Today's Date _____

What's special about today? _____

doodle

Nahum 1:7

The LORD is good, a strong hold in the day of trouble; and he knoweth them that trust in him.

NIGHT LIGHT

Today's Date _____

What's special about today? _____

doodle

John 8:12

Then spake Jesus again unto them, saying, I am the light of the world: he that followeth me shall not walk in darkness, but shall have the light of life.

NIGHT LIGHT

Today's Date _____

What's special about today? _____

doodle

Mark 10:27

And Jesus looking upon them saith, With men it is impossible, but not with God: for with God all things are possible.

NIGHT LIGHT

Today's Date _____

What's special about today? _____

doodle

Philippians 4:19

But my God shall supply all your needs according to his riches in glory by Christ Jesus.

NIGHT LIGHT

Today's Date _____

What's special about today? _____

doodle

Psalm 27:1

The Lord is my light and my salvation; whom shall I fear?
the Lord is the strength of my life; of whom shall I be afraid?

NIGHT LIGHT

Today's Date _____

What's special about today? _____

doodle

Psalm 16:8

I have set the Lord always before me: because
he is at my right hand, I shall not be moved.

NIGHT LIGHT

Today's Date _____

What's special about today? _____

doodle

Romans 8:38-39

For I am persuaded, that neither death, nor life, nor angels, nor principalities, nor powers, nor things present, nor things to come, Nor height, nor depth, nor any other creature, shall be able to separate us from the love of God, which is in Christ Jesus our Lord.

NIGHT LIGHT

Today's Date _____

What's special about today? _____

doodle

Isaiah 43:2

When thou passest through the waters, I will be with thee; and through the rivers, they shall not overflow thee: when thou walkest through the fire, thou shalt not be burned; neither shall the flame kindle upon thee.

NIGHT LIGHT

Today's Date _____

What's special about today? _____

doodle

Hebrews 11:1

Now faith is the substance of things hoped for, the evidence of things not seen

NIGHT LIGHT

Today's Date _____

What's special about today? _____

doodle

Jeremiah 29: 12-13

Then shall ye call upon me, and ye shall go and pray unto me, and I will hearken unto you. And ye shall seek me, and find me, when ye shall search for me with all your heart

NIGHT LIGHT

Today's Date _____

What's special about today? _____

doodle

John 14:19

Yet a little while, and the world seeth me no more; but ye see me:
because I live, ye shall live also

PSALM 145:18

NIGHT LIGHT

Today's Date _____

What's special about today? _____

doodle

2 Timothy 1:7

For God hath not given us the spirit of fear; but of power, and of love, and of a sound mind.

NIGHT LIGHT

Today's Date _____

What's special about today? _____

doodle

Psalm 9:9-10

The Lord also will be a refuge for the oppressed, a refuge in times of trouble. And they that know thy name will put their trust in thee: for thou, Lord, hast not forsaken them that seek thee.

NIGHT LIGHT

Today's Date _____

What's special about today? _____

doodle

Revelation 21:7

He that overcometh shall inherit all things; and I will be his God,
and he shall be my son.

NIGHT LIGHT

Today's Date _____

What's special about today? _____

doodle

2 Corinthians 4: 16-18

For which cause we faint not; but though our outward man perish, yet the inward man is renewed day by day. For our light affliction, which is but for a moment, worketh for us a far more exceeding and eternal weight of glory; While we look not at the things which are seen, but at the things which are not seen: for the things which are seen are temporal; but the things which are not seen are eternal.

NIGHT LIGHT

Today's Date _____

What's special about today? _____

doodle

Ephesians 4:2-3

With all lowliness and meekness, with longsuffering, forbearing one another in love; Endeavouring to keep the unity of the Spirit in the bond of peace

NIGHT LIGHT

Today's Date _____

What's special about today? _____

doodle

Psalm 145:9

The Lord is good to all: and his tender mercies are over all his works.

NIGHT LIGHT

Today's Date _____

What's special about today? _____

doodle

Titus 3:5

Not by works of righteousness which we have done, but according to his mercy he saved us, by the washing of regeneration, and renewing of the Holy Ghost

NIGHT LIGHT

Today's Date ———————

What's special about today? ———————————————————————————

doodle

Psalm 147: 3

He healeth the broken in heart, and bindeth up their wounds.

Today's Date _____

What's special about today? _____

doodle

Psalm 107:19

Then they cry unto the LORD in their trouble, and he saveth them out of their distresses.

Be strong

and of good courage.

fear not, nor be afraid of them:

for the Lord thy God, he it is that doth go with thee; *he will not fail thee, nor forsake thee.*

DEUTERONOMY 31:6

NIGHT LIGHT

Today's Date _____

What's special about today? _____

doodle

Psalm 30:10-12

Hear, O Lord, and have mercy upon me: Lord, be thou my helper. Thou hast turned for me my mourning into dancing: thou hast put off my sackcloth, and girded me with gladness; To the end that my glory may sing praise to thee, and not be silent. O Lord my God, I will give thanks unto thee for ever.

NIGHT LIGHT

Today's Date ──────

What's special about today? ──────────────────────────

doodle

Romans 15:13

Now the God of hope fill you with all joy and peace in believing, that ye may abound in hope, through the power of the Holy Ghost.

NIGHT LIGHT

Today's Date _____

What's special about today? _____

doodle

Isaiah 26:3-4

Thou wilt keep him in perfect peace, whose mind is stayed on thee: because he trusteth in thee. Trust ye in the LORD for ever: for in the LORD JEHOVAH is everlasting strength.

NIGHT  LIGHT

Today's Date ―――――――
What's special about today? ―――――――――――――――――――――

doodle

Psalm 34:8

O taste and see that the Lord is good: blessed is the man that trusteth in him.

NIGHT LIGHT

Today's Date _____

What's special about today? _____

doodle

2 Corinthians 1:3-4

Blessed be God, even the Father of our Lord Jesus Christ, the Father of mercies, and the God of all comfort; Who comforteth us in all our tribulation, that we may be able to comfort them which are in any trouble, by the comfort wherewith we ourselves are comforted of God.

NIGHT  LIGHT

Today's Date _____

What's special about today? _____

doodle

Ecclesiastes 3:1-4

To every thing there is a season, and a time to every purpose under the heaven: A time to be born, and a time to die; a time to plant, and a time to pluck up that which is planted; A time to kill, and a time to heal; a time to break down, and a time to build up; A time to weep, and a time to laugh; a time to mourn, and a time to dance

NIGHT  LIGHT

Today's Date _____

What's special about today? _____

doodle

Romans 8:31

What shall we then say to these things? If God be for us, who can be against us?

NIGHT LIGHT

Today's Date _____

What's special about today? _____

doodle

Psalm 46:1

God is our refuge and strength, a very present help in trouble.

NIGHT  LIGHT

Today's Date ─────────

What's special about today? ──────────────────────────

doodle

Psalm 37:23-24

The steps of a good man are ordered by the Lord: and he delighteth in his way. Though he fall, he shall not be utterly cast down: for the Lord upholdeth him with his hand.

Casting all your anxiety upon him, because he careth for you.

1 PETER 5:7 (ASV)

NIGHT LIGHT

Today's Date _____

What's special about today? _____

doodle

Hebrews 6:19

Which hope we have as an anchor of the soul, both sure and stedfast, and which entereth into that within the veil

NIGHT LIGHT

Today's Date —————

What's special about today? _____

doodle

Isaiah 41:10

Fear thou not; for I am with thee: be not dismayed; for I am thy God: I will strengthen thee; yea, I will help thee; yea, I will uphold thee with the right hand of my righteousness.

NIGHT LIGHT

Today's Date ──────

What's special about today? ──────────────────────

doodle

1 Corinthians 15:57

But thanks be to God, which giveth us the victory through our Lord Jesus Christ.

NIGHT  LIGHT

Today's Date _____

What's special about today? _____

doodle

Joshua 1:9

Have not I commanded thee? Be strong and of a good courage; be not afraid, neither be thou dismayed: for the Lord thy God is with thee whithersoever thou goest.

NIGHT LIGHT

Today's Date _____

What's special about today? _____

doodle

Romans 8:28

And we know that all things work together for good to them that love God,
to them who are the called according to his purpose.

NIGHT LIGHT

Today's Date ―――――

What's special about today? ―――――――――――――――――

doodle

Isaiah 49:13

Sing, O heavens; and be joyful, O earth; and break forth into singing, O mountains: for the Lord hath comforted his people, and will have mercy upon his afflicted.

NIGHT LIGHT

Today's Date _____

What's special about today? _____

doodle

Psalm 34:18

The Lord is nigh unto them that are of a broken heart; and saveth such as be of a contrite spirit.

NIGHT LIGHT

Today's Date _____

What's special about today? _____

doodle

Isaiah 40:29

He giveth power to the faint; and to them that have no might he increaseth strength.

NIGHT LIGHT

Today's Date _____

What's special about today? _____

doodle

2 Corinthians 5: 6-7

Therefore we are always confident, knowing that, whilst we are at home in the body, we are absent from the Lord: (For we walk by faith, not by sight)

 NIGHT LIGHT

Today's Date ―――――

What's special about today? ―――――――――――――――――――

doodle

1 Thessalonians 5: 16-18

Rejoice evermore. Pray without ceasing. In every thing give thanks: for this is the will of God in Christ Jesus concerning you.

NIGHT LIGHT

Today's Date _____

What's special about today? _____

doodle

Isaiah 43:1b

Fear not: for I have redeemed thee, I have called thee by thy name; thou art mine.

ISAIAH 40:31

But they that wait upon the Lord shall
renew their strength;
they shall mount up with
wings as eagles;
they shall run,
and not be weary;
and they shall
walk, and not faint.

NIGHT LIGHT

Today's Date _____

What's special about today? _____

doodle

Lamentations 3:22-23

It is of the Lord's mercies that we are not consumed, because his compassions fail not.
They are new every morning: great is thy faithfulness.

NIGHT LIGHT

Today's Date ——————

What's special about today? _____

doodle

1 Chronicles 16:11

Seek the Lord and his strength, seek his face continually.

NIGHT LIGHT

Today's Date _____

What's special about today? _____

doodle

Isaiah 33:2

O Lord, be gracious unto us; we have waited for thee: be thou their arm every morning, our salvation also in the time of trouble.

NIGHT LIGHT

Today's Date _____

What's special about today? _____

doodle

Ephesians 6: 10-11

Finally, my brethren, be strong in the Lord, and in the power of his might. Put on the whole armour of God, that ye may be able to stand against the wiles of the devil.

NIGHT LIGHT

Today's Date _____

What's special about today? _____

doodle

Psalm 30:10-12

Hear, O Lord, and have mercy upon me: Lord, be thou my helper. Thou hast turned for me my mourning into dancing: thou hast put off my sackcloth, and girded me with gladness; To the end that my glory may sing praise to thee, and not be silent. O Lord my God, I will give thanks unto thee for ever.

NIGHT LIGHT

Today's Date _____

What's special about today? _____

doodle

Colossians 3:13-15

Forbearing one another, and forgiving one another, if any man have a quarrel against any: even as Christ forgave you, so also do ye. And above all these things put on charity, which is the bond of perfectness. And let the peace of God rule in your hearts, to the which also ye are called in one body; and be ye thankful.

NIGHT LIGHT

Today's Date ──────────

What's special about today? ──────────────────────────────

doodle

1 Timothy 6:12

Fight the good fight of faith, lay hold on eternal life, whereunto thou art also called, and hast professed a good profession before many witnesses.

NIGHT LIGHT

Today's Date _____

What's special about today? _____

doodle

Matthew 7:9-11

Or what man is there of you, whom if his son ask bread, will he give him a stone? Or if he ask a fish, will he give him a serpent? If ye then, being evil, know how to give good gifts unto your children, how much more shall your Father which is in heaven give good things to them that ask him?

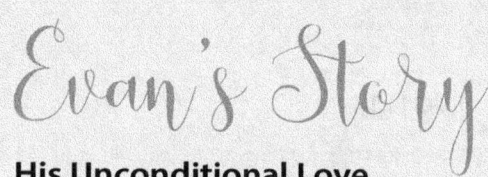
Evan's Story

His Unconditional Love

It was October 25, 2009, and I was working as a Labor & Delivery nurse. I was not assigned a specific patient that day; instead, I was a float nurse helping with several deliveries. I was so busy going from delivery to delivery that I had not stopped to eat, sit down, or take a break at all. Finally, it was time for me to take a very late lunch. Usually after a day like this, I would go to lunch, come back, and get a very easy assignment from the charge nurse, like a mom in early labor, so I could just relax for a bit.

As I turned the corner and walked by the nursing station, the charge nurse looked at me and immediately apologized, saying that we had a woman who needed to go for a C-section soon. The look in her eyes changed as she finished speaking, and I KNEW this look of heartbreak, as she told me this was a full-term baby who was not compatible with life and would likely not survive. There was no other nurse to take her back to the OR. I told the charge nurse I would take her but that I just needed a minute to eat something.

Whenever I got these assignments, I would just pray for the family and that I could meet their needs and simply love them in these moments. So, I ate and prayed.

Other nurses were already getting prepared for surgery as I walked into the room to meet Linda and Jim. They had kind smiles, and their eyes were full of both fear and excitement about meeting their son.

You see, they were told their son Evan would likely not make it through a vaginal birth. While you hear of so many women fearful and angry at having a C-section, Linda willfully chose and risked it all, just for the slightest chance her son might be born alive so she could spend every possible minute with him. To just see him alive was this family's hope.

She was all prepped, and the time had come to go back to the OR. Other staff and I were pushing the gurney down the hallway until we reached the point where we had to part with the family. They all gave each other hugs and love…the hope was palpable! They were all praying they could see Evan alive!

As we were in the hallway a few yards from the OR door, Linda quickly grabbed my forearm and said, "I've been praying for you!" I was stunned. I stopped and stared at her. I felt like she wanted me to see her, like really see her, and I did. She repeated herself and said, "I've been so excited, waiting and scared for this VERY moment, and I was praying that I'd have the right nurse here…and I do!" We both knew we were meant to be right there in THAT moment.

As I walked in the OR like I'd done hundreds of times, this time was different. I wanted so desperately for Linda and Jim to meet their son alive. I started praying too. Lord, PLEASE hear me! Please let Evan make it through this anesthesia and delivery! Please let him be born alive!

The procedure started, and as Evan was finally being delivered, there was complete silence. The NICU nursery team grabbed him directly off the abdomen from the surgeon's hands and rushed him to the infant warmer station to get to work. Still, silence filled the room. The team worked and worked, and I felt like I was holding my breath—this silence was crushing and felt like it lasted a lifetime. And then out of nowhere, we heard a little tiny squeak and the tiniest cry! As Evan fought for his breath, I think everyone in the room took a breath too!

Next came the moment I will never forget as Linda lay flat there on the OR table, just about ten feet away from her son. She turned her head back to get a glimpse of her baby boy as they continued to work on him. In true Cheerleader Mom fashion, she stretched out her hand to him and said, "Just do your best, Evan. Mommy loves you! Just do your best!" THAT MOMENT is etched in my mind forever. THAT is a picture of unconditional love. THOSE words of encouragement were so sweet to hear for everyone listening. See, it wasn't about what Linda wanted. She didn't tell Evan he had to live or survive to meet her needs, she just was encouraging him to do his best—whatever that looked like and no matter the outcome. She loved him unconditionally! Moments later, Evan was swaddled, brought to Linda and Jim, and placed in their arms to spend every minute they could with him.

Wow! What a reflection of God's heart. THIS is what LOVE looks like! Showing us He loves us right where we are, right in the moments we are struggling to even breathe! He never leaves us; His LOVE never leaves us. I feel like He says to each of us, "You are enough just the way you are. Just do your best. Daddy's right here with you!" He tells us He loves us, and He is our biggest cheerleader radiating love and words of encouragement to each one of us!

As the surgery came to an end, no one knew how long we'd have Evan, and his parents cherished every moment. The NICU team was happily surprised by the outcome, and we ended up going back to a private room for recovery to cherish and love on this precious gift.

Evan really did do his best, as he surpassed all expectations and lived for two days from October 25th to October 27th. It was more time than his family originally thought they'd have, but they still felt so robbed of the time they wanted with him.

I had the privilege of coming back on shift over the next days and taking care of Linda, Jim and Evan. I remember dressing Evan in a little moose onesie, wrapping him in multiple warm blankets, and laying him in a sweet bassinet as I prepared to take him to the morgue. Evan was born with six fingers and six toes on each hand and foot. I'll never forget when I met the security guard there. He was a young guy, heartbroken to see me meet him with a baby. He sat in silence for a moment, then said, "Boy, would he have been a good video gamer." I thought that was odd and strange at first, but then I realized he was staring at him in admiration for the beautiful way he was made. We can all see something different and beautiful in everything and in everyone we look at. We don't see things the same way, and what a blessing for that! To me, it was just another glimpse of the way God sees us. The world may tell us we are different or not enough, but God sees us and says, "I've made you perfectly—the EXACT way I wanted, and you are designed for my purpose and a reason. You are enough, and I love you the way you are!"

I am so thankful for Evan's entire family and the footprints they left on my heart. It took only two days to leave a lifetime impression, and what a complete honor it was for me to be a part of that journey. I'm so glad Linda prayed for me. I'm so glad God chose me that day to be a part of loving this family. I cannot wait to see Evan in Heaven!

nightlight

Today's Date _____

What's special about today? _____

Nahum 1:7

The LORD is good, a strong hold in the day of trouble;
and he knoweth them that trust in him.

Today's Date _____

What's special about today? _____

John 8:12

Then spake Jesus again unto them, saying, I am the light of the world: he that followeth me shall not walk in darkness, but shall have the light of life.

Today's Date _____

What's special about today? _____

Mark 10:27

And Jesus looking upon them saith, With men it is impossible, but not with God: for with God all things are possible.

Today's Date _____

What's special about today? _____

Philippians 4:19

But my God shall supply all your needs according to his riches in glory by Christ Jesus.

nightlight

Today's Date _____

What's special about today? _____

_____
_____
_____
_____
_____
_____
_____
_____
_____
_____
_____
_____
_____
_____
_____
_____
_____
_____
_____
_____
_____
_____
_____
_____
_____
_____
_____
_____

Psalm 27:1

The Lord is my light and my salvation; whom shall I fear? the Lord is the strength of my life; of whom shall I be afraid?

nightlight

Today's Date _____

What's special about today? _____

_____
_____
_____
_____
_____
_____
_____
_____
_____
_____
_____
_____
_____
_____
_____
_____
_____
_____
_____
_____
_____
_____
_____
_____
_____

Psalm 16:8

I have set the Lord always before me: because he is at my right hand, I shall not be moved.

Today's Date _____

What's special about today? _____

Romans 8:38-39

For I am persuaded, that neither death, nor life, nor angels, nor principalities, nor powers, nor things present, nor things to come, Nor height, nor depth, nor any other creature, shall be able to separate us from the love of God, which is in Christ Jesus our Lord.

Today's Date _____

What's special about today? _____

Isaiah 43:2

When thou passest through the waters, I will be with thee; and through the rivers, they shall not overflow thee: when thou walkest through the fire, thou shalt not be burned; neither shall the flame kindle upon thee.

nightlight

Today's Date _____

What's special about today? _____

_____
_____
_____
_____
_____
_____
_____
_____
_____
_____
_____
_____
_____
_____
_____
_____
_____
_____
_____
_____
_____
_____
_____
_____
_____
_____

Hebrews 11:1

Now faith is the substance of things hoped for, the evidence of things not seen

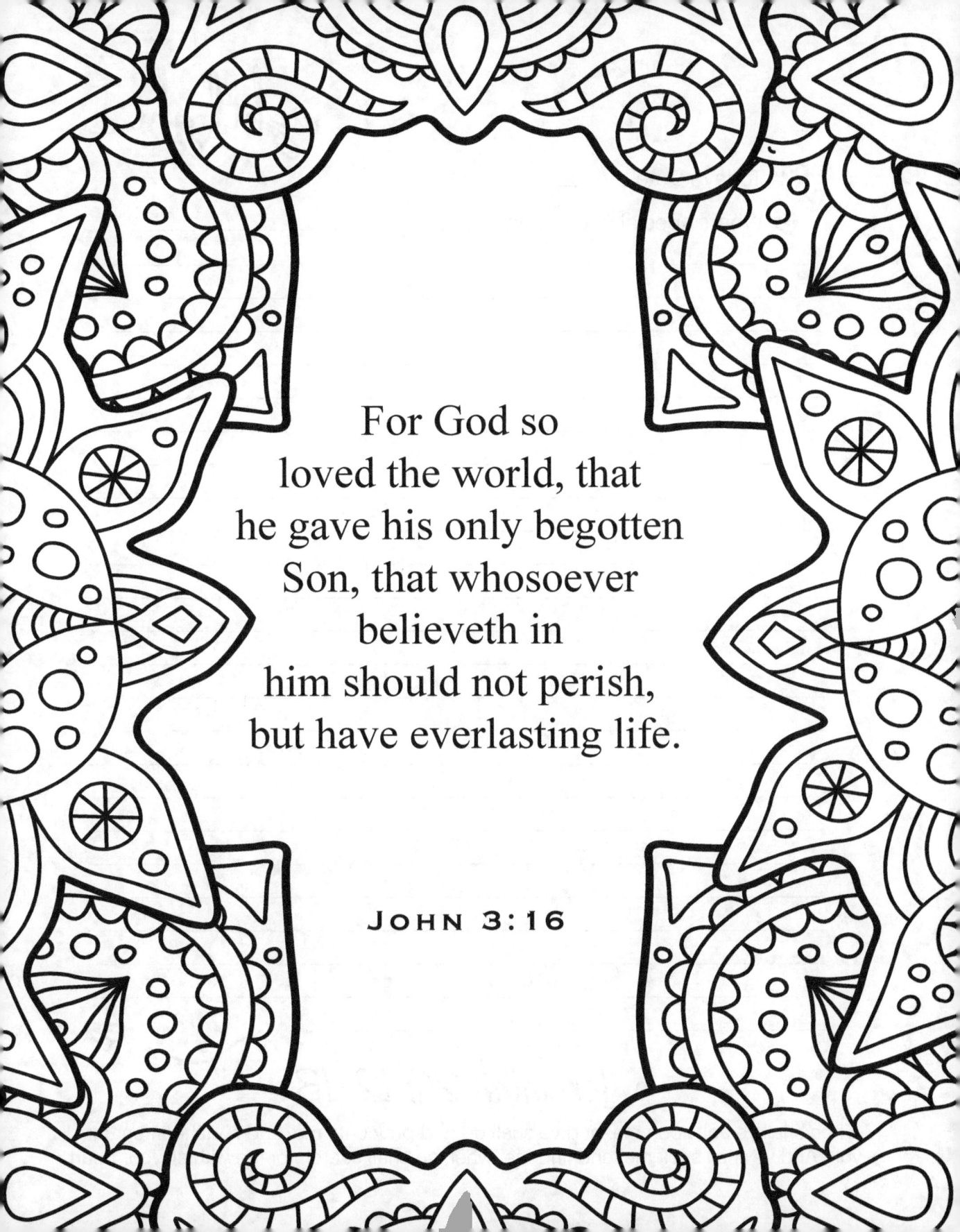

Today's Date _____

What's special about today? _____

Jeremiah 29: 12-13

Then shall ye call upon me, and ye shall go and pray unto me, and I will hearken unto you. And ye shall seek me, and find me, when ye shall search for me with all your heart

Today's Date _____

What's special about today? _____

John 14:19

Yet a little while, and the world seeth me no more; but ye see me: because I live, ye shall live also

nightlight

- Today's Date _____
- What's special about today? _____

2 Timothy 1:7

For God hath not given us the spirit of fear; but of power,
and of love, and of a sound mind.

♡♡ Today's Date _____
♡ What's special about today? _____

_____
_____
_____
_____
_____
_____
_____
_____
_____
_____
_____
_____
_____
_____
_____
_____
_____
_____
_____
_____
_____
_____
_____
_____
_____
_____
_____
_____

Psalm 9:9-10

The Lord also will be a refuge for the oppressed, a refuge in times of trouble. And they that know thy name will put their trust in thee: for thou, Lord, hast not forsaken them that seek thee.

nightlight

Today's Date _____

What's special about today? _____

_____
_____
_____
_____
_____
_____
_____
_____
_____
_____
_____
_____
_____
_____
_____
_____
_____
_____
_____
_____
_____
_____
_____

Revelation 21:7

He that overcometh shall inherit all things;
and I will be his God, and he shall be my son.

Today's Date _____

What's special about today? _____

2 Corinthians 4: 16-18

For which cause we faint not; but though our outward man perish, yet the inward man is renewed day by day. For our light affliction, which is but for a moment, worketh for us a far more exceeding and eternal weight of glory; While we look not at the things which are seen, but at the things which are not seen: for the things which are seen are temporal; but the things which are not seen are eternal.

nightlight

♡ Today's Date _____
♡ What's special about today? _____

Ephesians 4:2-3

With all lowliness and meekness, with longsuffering, forbearing one another in love;
Endeavouring to keep the unity of the Spirit in the bond of peace

nightlight

Today's Date _____

What's special about today? _____

Psalm 145:9

The Lord is good to all: and his tender mercies are over all his works.

Today's Date _____

What's special about today? _____

Titus 3:5

Not by works of righteousness which we have done, but according to his mercy he saved us, by the washing of regeneration, and renewing of the Holy Ghost

Today's Date _____

What's special about today? _____

Psalm 147:3

He healeth the broken in heart, and bindeth up their wounds.

nightlight

Today's Date _____

What's special about today? _____

_____
_____
_____
_____
_____
_____
_____
_____
_____
_____
_____
_____
_____
_____
_____
_____
_____
_____
_____
_____
_____
_____
_____
_____
_____
_____
_____
_____

Psalm 107:19

Then they cry unto the LORD in their trouble,
and he saveth them out of their distresses.

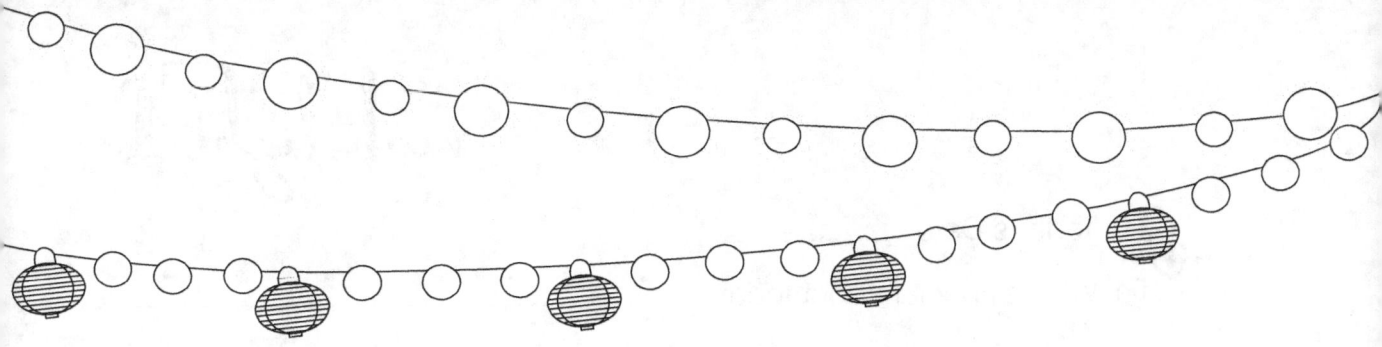

I am the light of the world: he that followeth me shall not walk in darkness, but shall have the light of life.

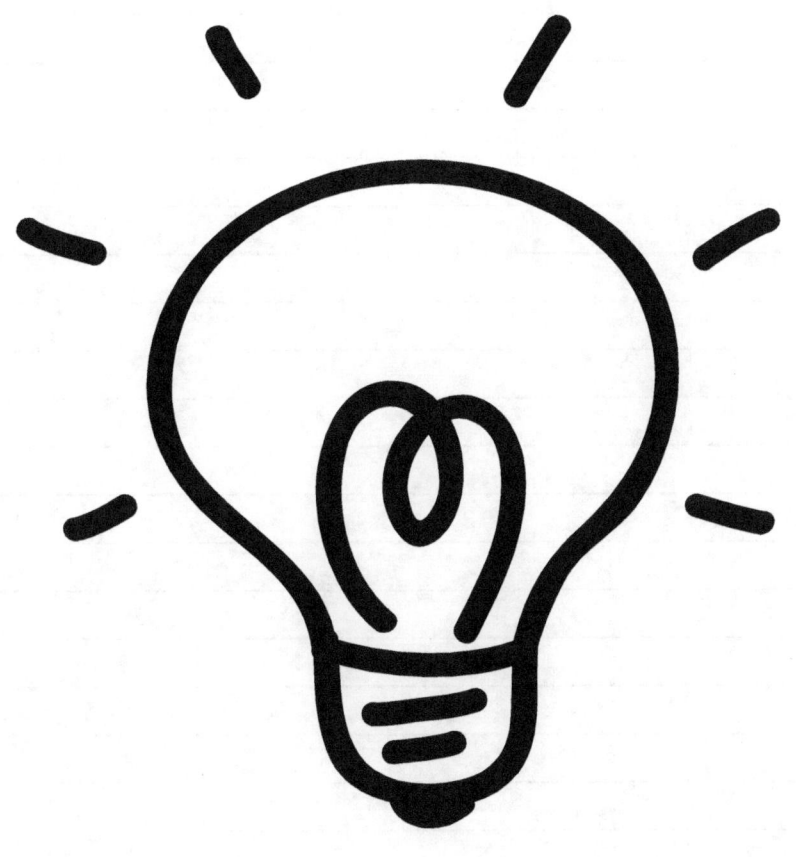

John 8:12

Today's Date _____

What's special about today? _____

_____
_____
_____
_____
_____
_____
_____
_____
_____
_____
_____
_____
_____
_____
_____
_____
_____
_____
_____
_____
_____
_____
_____
_____
_____

Psalm 30:10-12

Hear, O Lord, and have mercy upon me: Lord, be thou my helper. Thou hast turned for me my mourning into dancing: thou hast put off my sackcloth, and girded me with gladness; To the end that my glory may sing praise to thee, and not be silent. O Lord my God, I will give thanks unto thee for ever.

nightlight

Today's Date _____

What's special about today? _____

Romans 15:13

Now the God of hope fill you with all joy and peace in believing,
that ye may abound in hope, through the power of the Holy Ghost.

nightlight

- Today's Date _____
- What's special about today? _____

Isaiah 26:3-4

Thou wilt keep him in perfect peace, whose mind is stayed on thee: because he trusteth in thee. Trust ye in the LORD for ever: for in the LORD JEHOVAH is everlasting strength.

nightlight

Today's Date _____

What's special about today? _____

Psalm 34:8

O taste and see that the Lord is good: blessed is the man that trusteth in him.

Today's Date _____

What's special about today? _____

2 Corinthians 1:3-4

Blessed be God, even the Father of our Lord Jesus Christ, the Father of mercies, and the God of all comfort; Who comforteth us in all our tribulation, that we may be able to comfort them which are in any trouble, by the comfort wherewith we ourselves are comforted of God.

Today's Date _____

What's special about today? _____

Ecclesiastes 3:1-4

To every thing there is a season, and a time to every purpose under the heaven: A time to be born, and a time to die; a time to plant, and a time to pluck up that which is planted; A time to kill, and a time to heal; a time to break down, and a time to build up; A time to weep, and a time to laugh; a time to mourn, and a time to dance

nightlight

♡ Today's Date _____
♡ What's special about today? _____

Romans 8:31

What shall we then say to these things? If God be for us, who can be against us?

nightlight

Today's Date _____

What's special about today? _____

Psalm 46:1

God is our refuge and strength, a very present help in trouble

Today's Date _____

What's special about today? _____

Psalm 37:23-24

The steps of a good man are ordered by the Lord: and he delighteth in his way. Though he fall, he shall not be utterly cast down: for the Lord upholdeth him with his hand.

nightlight

Today's Date _____

What's special about today? _____

Hebrews 6:19

Which hope we have as an anchor of the soul, both sure and stedfast, and which entereth into that within the veil

Today's Date _____

What's special about today? _____

Isaiah 41:10

Fear thou not; for I am with thee: be not dismayed; for I am thy God: I will strengthen thee; yea, I will help thee; yea, I will uphold thee with the right hand of my righteousness.

Today's Date _____

What's special about today? _____

1 Corinthians 15:57

But thanks be to God, which giveth us the victory through our Lord Jesus Christ.

Today's Date _____

What's special about today? _____

Joshua 1:9

Have not I commanded thee? Be strong and of a good courage; be not afraid, neither be thou dismayed: for the Lord thy God is with thee whithersoever thou goest.

nightlight

♡ Today's Date _____
♡ What's special about today? _____

Romans 8:28

And we know that all things work together for good to them that love God,
to them who are the called according to his purpose.

Today's Date _____

What's special about today? _____

Isaiah 49:13

Sing, O heavens; and be joyful, O earth; and break forth into singing, O mountains: for the Lord hath comforted his people, and will have mercy upon his afflicted.

nightlight

Today's Date _____

What's special about today? _____

_____
_____
_____
_____
_____
_____
_____
_____
_____
_____
_____
_____
_____
_____
_____
_____
_____
_____
_____
_____
_____
_____
_____
_____
_____
_____

Psalm 34:18

The Lord is nigh unto them that are of a broken heart; and saveth such as be of a contrite spirit.

Today's Date _____

What's special about today? _____

Isaiah 40:29

He giveth power to the faint; and to them that have no might he increaseth strength.

nightlight

♡♡ Today's Date _____
♡ What's special about today? _____

2 Corinthians 5: 6-7

Therefore we are always confident, knowing that, whilst we are at home in the body, we are absent from the Lord: (For we walk by faith, not by sight)

Today's Date _____

What's special about today? _____

1 Thessalonians 5: 16-18

Rejoice evermore. Pray without ceasing. In every thing give thanks: for this is the will of God in Christ Jesus concerning you.

nightlight

Today's Date _____

What's special about today? _____

_____
_____
_____
_____
_____
_____
_____
_____
_____
_____
_____
_____
_____
_____
_____
_____
_____
_____
_____
_____
_____
_____
_____
_____
_____

Isaiah 43:1b

Fear not: for I have redeemed thee, I have called thee by thy name; thou art mine.

These things I have spoken unto you,
that in me ye might have peace. In the
world ye shall have tribulation, but be of good cheer,
I have overcome the world.

JOHN 16:33

nightlight

Today's Date _____

What's special about today? _____

Lamentations 3:22-23

It is of the Lord's mercies that we are not consumed, because his compassions fail not.
They are new every morning: great is thy faithfulness.

Today's Date _____

What's special about today? _____

1 Chronicles 16:11

Seek the Lord and his strength, seek his face continually.

Today's Date _____

What's special about today? _____

Isaiah 33:2

O Lord, be gracious unto us; we have waited for thee: be thou their arm every morning, our salvation also in the time of trouble.

- Today's Date _____
- What's special about today? _____

Ephesians 6: 10-11

Finally, my brethren, be strong in the Lord, and in the power of his might. Put on the whole armour of God, that ye may be able to stand against the wiles of the devil.

Today's Date _____

What's special about today? _____

Psalm 30:10-12

Hear, O Lord, and have mercy upon me: Lord, be thou my helper. Thou hast turned for me my mourning into dancing: thou hast put off my sackcloth, and girded me with gladness; To the end that my glory may sing praise to thee, and not be silent. O Lord my God, I will give thanks unto thee for ever.

Today's Date _____

What's special about today? _____

Colossians 3:13-15

Forbearing one another, and forgiving one another, if any man have a quarrel against any: even as Christ forgave you, so also do ye. And above all these things put on charity, which is the bond of perfectness. And let the peace of God rule in your hearts, to the which also ye are called in one body; and be ye thankful.

Today's Date _____

What's special about today? _____

---

1 Timothy 6:12

Fight the good fight of faith, lay hold on eternal life, whereunto thou art also called, and hast professed a good profession before many witnesses.

Today's Date _____

What's special about today? _____

Matthew 7:9-11

Or what man is there of you, whom if his son ask bread, will he give him a stone? Or if he ask a fish, will he give him a serpent? If ye then, being evil, know how to give good gifts unto your children, how much more shall your Father which is in heaven give good things to them that ask him?

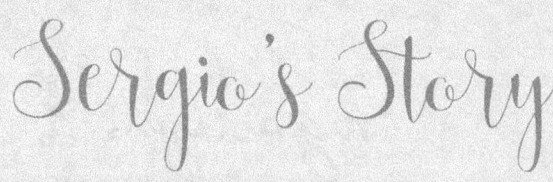

Sergio's Story

He Never Leaves You

My husband, Sergio lost his two brothers, Danny (aged twelve) and Kristopher (aged four), and his mom, Elisa (aged twenty-eight) in a car accident when he was only eight years old.

They were on the way to his soccer game early one morning and were suddenly hit by a driver who was both drunk and high. The other car T-boned the passenger side door where Sergio's mom and brothers were sitting. Sergio was sleeping in the seat behind his dad, Armando, who was driving the car.

Sergio was not hurt, so after the ambulance took the family to the hospital, hospital staff and nurses placed him in a separate room to wait by himself. The staff was instructed not to turn on the TV. You see, while Sergio waited in this room, his mother died in surgery, his brother Danny was brain dead and being put on a ventilator, and his dad was still in surgery, fighting for his life. His little brother Kristopher had died at the scene of the accident. Sergio's father remembers the doctors talking around him, saying how he was not going to live. He remembers the priest coming in and giving him his last rites.

A new RN at shift change came in and saw this bored little boy waiting in the room all by himself and felt bad for him, so she turned on the TV. This is how Sergio found out his family was dead. The news actually reported inaccurately that his entire family died, and he was the only survivor.

Sergio doesn't remember this next part exactly, only stories of what others would recall and tell him later. He was so distraught when he saw the news of his family's death on TV, he tried to jump out of the hospital window. Thankfully, the nurses and staff were able to stop him.

Hard decisions had to be made, and no one wanted to make the decision on what to do about Danny being on the ventilator. Should they keep him on it longer? Should they discontinue it? They ended up waiting for two months when Armando was able to make a decision. They pulled the plug and let Danny pass away.

During this time, Sergio went to live with his cousins. He was carrying guilt about the accident that no one knew about. This little eight-year-old boy thought the accident was all his fault because he had forgotten his soccer shoes. The family had left that morning to go to his soccer game, but they had to turn around to go back for Sergio's soccer shoes that he had forgotten. Thoughts ran through Sergio's little mind... *Did I just kill my family? Would they all be alive if I had just remembered my shoes that morning? Would we have been in that intersection if I had not forgotten them?*

An eight-year-old who just lost his whole world could not see the truth—that this was NOT his fault. He could not see that the SOLE cause of this tragic loss rests on the shoulders of a young man who was drunk and high, who made really bad decisions that day. So, Sergio lived in grief and guilt alone for many years, believing lies that were never true and carrying a burden that was never his to carry.

Months later when Sergio's dad, Armando, got out of the hospital, he was also guilt-ridden—the guilt of being the driver, the pain and emotions of losing his beloved wife and two sons, the physical pain from rehab to learn how to walk again and how to eat/feed himself again. Learning how to perform basic daily functions on his own was just too overwhelming. One night, Armando grabbed his gun, loaded it, and went to Sergio's bedroom as he slept. He put a pillow over Sergio's head and was going to shoot him and then shoot himself to finally end this nightmare.

This right here—THIS MOMENT! —I believe is a moment of divine intervention by God. This pain-stricken, broken moment I am beyond thankful for! As Armando stands over his precious child's bed, broken-hearted, desperate, and deep in grief, he does not want to live any longer. As he lifts his gun, ready "to just go be with his family and stop the pain," he has a moment of clarity. He realizes he cannot do this to Sergio, and resolves they must keep living.

In that moment of courage and strength to keep going despite the pain, I fully believe it was divine help from God. We all hear from God. He speaks to each of us differently. (Ezekiel 2:1; 1 Corinthians 3:16). Some call it your conscience or a little internal nudge. I believe sometimes He speaks to us in a quiet voice, and other times He screams to get our attention.

Armando was mad. He was angry at God. I believe it was the gentle voice of God speaking through clarity of thought during that moment. A small inner voice of the Lord saying, "I love you, Armando. I'm in mourning with you, Armando. I love you and I won't leave you, Armando." His promises are personal. One I hold dearly is God says He will never leave us or forsake us. (Deut: 31:8)

Armando would only share this story with me just a few short years ago, almost three decades after this incident. Sergio had never known this story until then, and he felt uncomfortable as he heard it. Armando spent so many years being angry and hating God for taking his family. I love that no matter how angry or hurt we are, God still chases after us, loves on us, and still speaks to us even when we try to reject Him. He is fighting for you! (Exodus 14:14)

I heard someone say once that God is not the author of evil and pain, but instead, He mourns with us during our losses. Your choices matter! Because Armando chose to listen amidst the hurt, pain, and chaos in his body and mind, Sergio is alive. Because of this one choice, I have a wonderful husband, three beautiful children, and lives are changed because he is here today. Generations will exist because of this choice and a legacy of love. Be encouraged that your story is not fully written yet. There is a God who loves you unconditionally. He is for you and He knows your name!

NIGHT LIGHT

Today's Date _____

What's special about today? _____

doodle

Nahum 1:7

The LORD is good, a strong hold in the day of trouble; and he knoweth them that trust in him.

NIGHT LIGHT

Today's Date _____

What's special about today? _____

doodle

John 8:12

Then spake Jesus again unto them, saying, I am the light of the world: he that followeth me shall not walk in darkness, but shall have the light of life.

NIGHT LIGHT

Today's Date _____

What's special about today? _____

doodle

Mark 10:27

And Jesus looking upon them saith, With men it is impossible,
but not with God: for with God all things are possible.

NIGHT LIGHT

Today's Date _____

What's special about today? _____

doodle

Philippians 4:19

But my God shall supply all your needs according to his riches in glory by Christ Jesus.

NIGHT LIGHT

Today's Date _____

What's special about today? _____

doodle

Psalm 27:1

The Lord is my light and my salvation; whom shall I fear?
the Lord is the strength of my life; of whom shall I be afraid?

NIGHT LIGHT

Today's Date ———————

What's special about today? _____

doodle

Psalm 16:8

I have set the Lord always before me: because
he is at my right hand, I shall not be moved.

NIGHT LIGHT

Today's Date ―――――――

What's special about today? ―――――――――――――――――――――

doodle

Romans 8:38-39

For I am persuaded, that neither death, nor life, nor angels, nor principalities, nor powers, nor things present, nor things to come, Nor height, nor depth, nor any other creature, shall be able to separate us from the love of God, which is in Christ Jesus our Lord.

NIGHT LIGHT

Today's Date ——————

What's special about today? ——————————————————————

doodle

Isaiah 43:2

When thou passest through the waters, I will be with thee; and through the rivers, they shall not overflow thee: when thou walkest through the fire, thou shalt not be burned; neither shall the flame kindle upon thee.

NIGHT LIGHT

Today's Date _____

What's special about today? _____

doodle

Hebrews 11:1

Now faith is the substance of things hoped for, the evidence of things not seen

NIGHT LIGHT

Today's Date ―――――――

What's special about today? ――――――――――――――――――――――

doodle

Jeremiah 29: 12-13

Then shall ye call upon me, and ye shall go and pray unto me, and I will hearken unto you. And ye shall seek me, and find me, when ye shall search for me with all your heart

NIGHT LIGHT

Today's Date _____

What's special about today? _____

doodle

John 14:19

Yet a little while, and the world seeth me no more; but ye see me:
because I live, ye shall live also

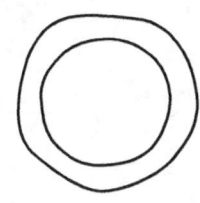

Come unto me, all ye that labour and are heavy laden, and I will give you rest.
Take my yoke upon you, and learn of me;
for I am meek and lowly in heart:
and ye shall find rest unto your souls.
For my yoke is easy, and
my burden is light.

MATTHEW 11:28-30

NIGHT LIGHT

Today's Date _____

What's special about today? _____

doodle

2 Timothy 1:7

For God hath not given us the spirit of fear; but of power, and of love, and of a sound mind.

NIGHT LIGHT

Today's Date ―――――――

What's special about today? ―――――――――――――――――――――――――

doodle

Psalm 9:9-10

The Lord also will be a refuge for the oppressed, a refuge in times of trouble. And they that know thy name will put their trust in thee: for thou, Lord, hast not forsaken them that seek thee.

NIGHT LIGHT

Today's Date ──────────

What's special about today? ──────────────────────────────

doodle

Revelation 21:7

He that overcometh shall inherit all things; and I will be his God, and he shall be my son.

NIGHT LIGHT

Today's Date _____

What's special about today? _____

doodle

2 Corinthians 4: 16-18

For which cause we faint not; but though our outward man perish, yet the inward man is renewed day by day. For our light affliction, which is but for a moment, worketh for us a far more exceeding and eternal weight of glory; While we look not at the things which are seen, but at the things which are not seen: for the things which are seen are temporal; but the things which are not seen are eternal.

NIGHT  LIGHT

Today's Date ─────────

What's special about today? ────────────────────────

doodle

Ephesians 4:2-3

With all lowliness and meekness, with longsuffering, forbearing one another in love; Endeavouring to keep the unity of the Spirit in the bond of peace

NIGHT LIGHT

Today's Date _____

What's special about today? _____

doodle

Psalm 145:9

The Lord is good to all: and his tender mercies are over all his works.

NIGHT LIGHT

Today's Date ―――――――

What's special about today? ――――――――――――――――――――

doodle

Titus 3:5

Not by works of righteousness which we have done, but according to his mercy
he saved us, by the washing of regeneration, and renewing of the Holy Ghost

NIGHT   LIGHT

Today's Date ─────────

What's special about today? ──────────────────────────

doodle

Psalm 147: 3

He healeth the broken in heart, and bindeth up their wounds.

NIGHT LIGHT

Today's Date _____

What's special about today? _____

doodle

Psalm 107:19

Then they cry unto the LORD in their trouble, and he saveth them out of their distresses.

Philippians 4:6-7 (ASV)

In nothing be anxious; but in everything by prayer and supplication with **THANKSGIVING**

LET YOUR REQUESTS BE MADE KNOWN UNTO GOD.

And the peace of God, which passeth all understanding, shall guard your hearts and your thoughts in Christ Jesus.

NIGHT LIGHT

Today's Date _____

What's special about today? _____

doodle

Psalm 30:10-12

Hear, O Lord, and have mercy upon me: Lord, be thou my helper. Thou hast turned for me my mourning into dancing: thou hast put off my sackcloth, and girded me with gladness; To the end that my glory may sing praise to thee, and not be silent.
O Lord my God, I will give thanks unto thee for ever.

NIGHT  LIGHT

Today's Date ———————

What's special about today? ————————————————————————

doodle

Romans 15:13

Now the God of hope fill you with all joy and peace in believing, that ye may abound in hope, through the power of the Holy Ghost.

NIGHT LIGHT

Today's Date _____

What's special about today? _____

doodle

Isaiah 26:3-4

Thou wilt keep him in perfect peace, whose mind is stayed on thee: because he trusteth in thee. Trust ye in the LORD for ever: for in the LORD JEHOVAH is everlasting strength.

NIGHT LIGHT

Today's Date ─────────

What's special about today? ────────────────────────────────

doodle

Psalm 34:8

O taste and see that the Lord is good: blessed is the man that trusteth in him.

NIGHT LIGHT

Today's Date _____

What's special about today? _____

doodle

2 Corinthians 1:3-4

Blessed be God, even the Father of our Lord Jesus Christ, the Father of mercies, and the God of all comfort; Who comforteth us in all our tribulation, that we may be able to comfort them which are in any trouble, by the comfort wherewith we ourselves are comforted of God.

 NIGHT LIGHT

Today's Date _____

What's special about today? _____

doodle

Ecclesiastes 3:1-4

To every thing there is a season, and a time to every purpose under the heaven: A time to be born, and a time to die; a time to plant, and a time to pluck up that which is planted; A time to kill, and a time to heal; a time to break down, and a time to build up; A time to weep, and a time to laugh; a time to mourn, and a time to dance

NIGHT  LIGHT

Today's Date ──────

What's special about today? ────────────────────

```
_____
_____
_____
_____
_____
_____
_____
_____
_____
_____
_____
_____
_____
_____
_____
_____
_____
_____
```

doodle

Romans 8:31

What shall we then say to these things? If God be for us, who can be against us?

NIGHT LIGHT

Today's Date _____

What's special about today? _____

doodle

Psalm 46:1

God is our refuge and strength, a very present help in trouble.

 NIGHT LIGHT

Today's Date ─────────

What's special about today? ─────────────────────────

doodle

Psalm 37:23-24

The steps of a good man are ordered by the Lord: and he delighteth in his way. Though he fall, he shall not be utterly cast down: for the Lord upholdeth him with his hand.

NIGHT LIGHT

Today's Date _____

What's special about today? _____

doodle

Joshua 1:9

Have not I commanded thee? Be strong and of a good courage; be not afraid, neither be thou dismayed: for the Lord thy God is with thee whithersoever thou goest.

NIGHT LIGHT

Today's Date _____

What's special about today? _____

doodle

Romans 8:28

And we know that all things work together for good to them that love God,
to them who are the called according to his purpose.

NIGHT LIGHT

Today's Date ———————

What's special about today? ——————————————————————————

doodle

Isaiah 49:13

Sing, O heavens; and be joyful, O earth; and break forth into singing, O mountains: for the Lord hath comforted his people, and will have mercy upon his afflicted.

NIGHT LIGHT

Today's Date ──────

What's special about today? ──────────────────────

doodle

Psalm 34:18

The Lord is nigh unto them that are of a broken heart; and saveth such as be of a contrite spirit.

NIGHT LIGHT

Today's Date _____

What's special about today? _____

doodle

Isaiah 40:29

He giveth power to the faint; and to them that have no might he increaseth strength.

NIGHT  LIGHT

Today's Date ―――――

What's special about today? ――――――――――――――――――

doodle

2 Corinthians 5: 6-7

Therefore we are always confident, knowing that, whilst we are at home in the body,
we are absent from the Lord: (For we walk by faith, not by sight)

NIGHT LIGHT

Today's Date _____

What's special about today? _____

doodle

1 Thessalonians 5: 16-18

Rejoice evermore. Pray without ceasing. In every thing give thanks: for this is the will of God in Christ Jesus concerning you.

NIGHT LIGHT

Today's Date _____

What's special about today? _____

doodle

Isaiah 43:1b

Fear not: for I have redeemed thee, I have called thee by thy name; thou art mine.

NIGHT LIGHT

Today's Date _____

What's special about today? _____

doodle

Lamentations 3:22-23

It is of the Lord's mercies that we are not consumed, because his compassions fail not.
They are new every morning: great is thy faithfulness.

NIGHT LIGHT

Today's Date _____

What's special about today? _____

doodle

1 Chronicles 16:11

Seek the Lord and his strength, seek his face continually.

NIGHT LIGHT

Today's Date _____

What's special about today? _____

doodle

Isaiah 33:2

O Lord, be gracious unto us; we have waited for thee: be thou their arm every morning, our salvation also in the time of trouble.

NIGHT LIGHT

Today's Date _____

What's special about today? _____

_____
_____
_____
_____
_____
_____
_____
_____
_____
_____
_____
_____
_____
_____
_____
_____
_____
_____
_____

doodle

Ephesians 6: 10-11

Finally, my brethren, be strong in the Lord, and in the power of his might. Put on the whole armour of God, that ye may be able to stand against the wiles of the devil.

NIGHT LIGHT

Today's Date _____

What's special about today? _____

doodle

Psalm 30:10-12

Hear, O Lord, and have mercy upon me: Lord, be thou my helper. Thou hast turned for me my mourning into dancing: thou hast put off my sackcloth, and girded me with gladness; To the end that my glory may sing praise to thee, and not be silent. O Lord my God, I will give thanks unto thee for ever.

NIGHT LIGHT

Today's Date ——————

What's special about today? ——————————————————————

doodle

Colossians 3:13-15

Forbearing one another, and forgiving one another, if any man have a quarrel against any: even as Christ forgave you, so also do ye. And above all these things put on charity, which is the bond of perfectness. And let the peace of God rule in your hearts, to the which also ye are called in one body; and be ye thankful.

NIGHT LIGHT

Today's Date _____

What's special about today? _____

doodle

1 Timothy 6:12

Fight the good fight of faith, lay hold on eternal life, whereunto thou art also called, and hast professed a good profession before many witnesses.

NIGHT LIGHT

Today's Date _____

What's special about today? _____

doodle

Matthew 7:9-11

Or what man is there of you, whom if his son ask bread, will he give him a stone? Or if he ask a fish, will he give him a serpent? If ye then, being evil, know how to give good gifts unto your children, how much more shall your Father which is in heaven give good things to them that ask him?

NIGHT  LIGHT

Today's Date _____

What's special about today? _____

doodle

Hebrews 6:19

Which hope we have as an anchor of the soul, both sure and stedfast, and which entereth into that within the veil

I don't believe you are reading this by accident. I believe in divine appointments, and I know God has something amazing to show you and speak to you during this time.

He loves you, He knows your name, and He is ready to meet you right where you are! Truth is, He already knows how you feel; He is eagerly waiting for you to talk to Him and tell Him yourself. I pray blessings upon blessings over you, and pray a supernatural peace rests upon you.

Numbers 6:24 - 26
The Lord bless thee, and keep thee:
The Lord make his face shine upon thee, and be gracious unto thee:
The Lord lift up his countenance upon thee, and give thee peace

www.ingramcontent.com/pod-product-compliance
Lightning Source LLC
Chambersburg PA
CBHW081112080526
44587CB00021B/3558